Sid's Sailing Days:
The Log of the Reine D'Avor

Sid's Sailing Days: The Log of the Reine D'Avor

Thomas Mariner

2016

Copyright © 2016 Thomas Mariner

All rights reserved. This book or any portion thereof may not be reproduced or used in any manner whatsoever without the express written permission of the publisher except for the use of brief quotations in a book review or scholarly journal.

First Printing: 2016

ISBN 978-1-326-48654-9

Dedication

This book is to all intrepid mariners: men & women throughout history drawn to the blue horizon not just to challenge sea & swell, but with belief that 'tomorrow' is waiting over the crest of the wave.

Our father Sid Jobbins wrote this diary aboard the Reine D'Avor in 1938, with whittled pencil & quiet belief -

***In Memoriam**:*

Sidney Thomas Jobbins   1911-2001

...thank you dad

On August 25th 1938, the 'Reine d'Avor' sailing yacht left Jersey, bound for Barbados & Australia; aboard her ten people: HH Brache (the Skipper), his wife and family, and five seafarers – George Harris, Arthur Kennard, Tony Lee, Sid Jobbins and Fred Rebell (First Mate).

An original Collins 1938 Royal Diary is the source document: compiled by
Sid Jobbins in lead pencil every day of the voyage; you will read a full & complete transcript of the diary log, with photographic records of the journey & crew.

                                                cont.d

Amongst the crew we find First Mate **Fred Rebell**, who came to this voyage acclaimed as '***first man to cross the Pacific 9,000 miles from west to east in an open-boat single-handed crossing'***: he continued this voyage with the Brache family to Sydney, Australia, via the Panama Canal arriving on 15 December 1939.

October 20th 1938, next attempt,

"Rebell & myself repairing balloon jib sail in the North East Trades,

about 300 miles from Barbados"

W. Harkes

... Sid's text on front photo

Welcome aboard to a dynamic snapshot of life at sea, and a mariner's view of world events 1938; told with inimitable wit & humor, it reveals the courage and resilience of every sailor who ever stepped off dry-land & set sail for the unknown.

Sid returned to the UK, married with family, grandchildren & great-grandchildren... & although land-based, in quieter moments with a twinkle in his eye and a wry smile, he would be there... running free, with big blue seas astern; sun shining, a fair breeze, and the Tunny fish jumping...'

Americas Cup 2016 Edition

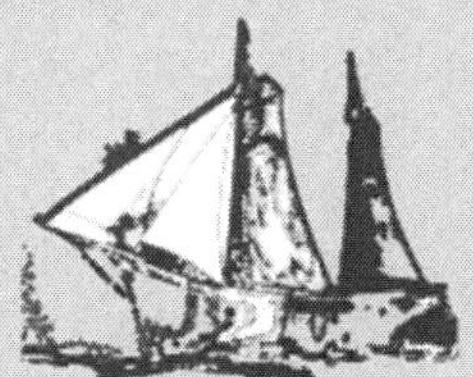

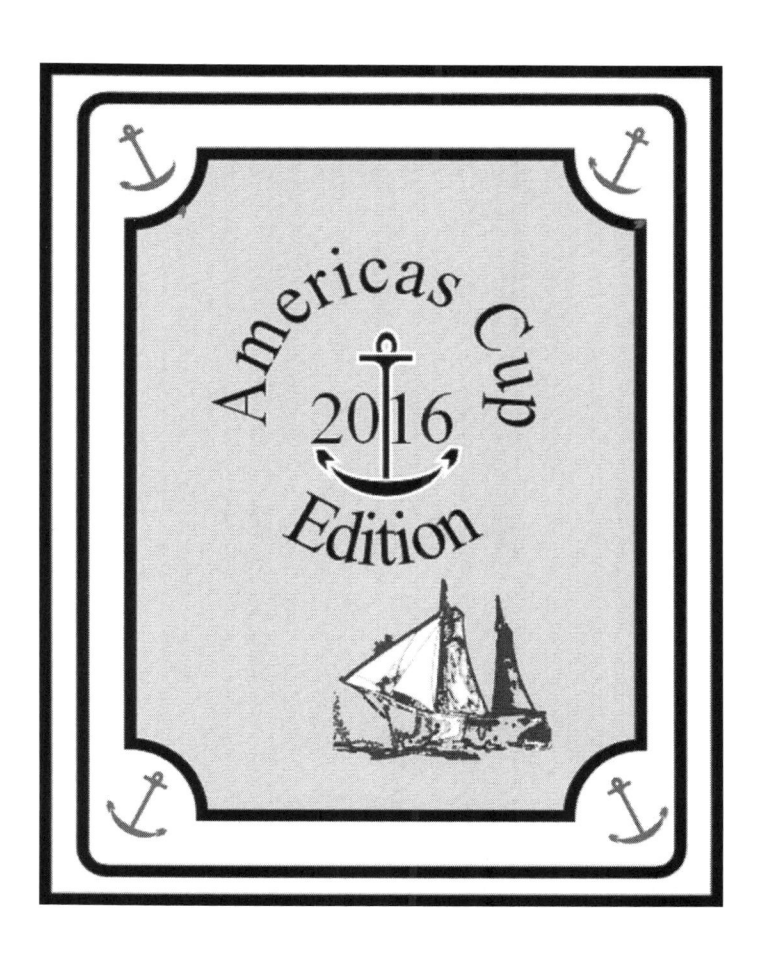

August 1938   Tuesday 16

DIARY BEGINS

Left Jersey on SR Brittany for St. Malo France 7.30am
Arrive St. Malo 10.30 am
Met by the Skipper and Mr. Woodwards
I was very pleased to see them,
Sent my gear on to our ship at Cancale and then...
The three of us walk about St Malo, settling things up for the trip

Cancale is about 8 miles from St Malo.
Well, we darn near walked our feet off, but the Skipper got things settled at last.
We left St Malo about 6 pm and bussed to Cancale,
Cancale is a very nice little town, most of the men here are fishermen.
The ship looks good to me, they have painted her bottom with bitchumastix black,

The Log of the Reine D'Avor

August 1938   **cont.d Tuesday 16**

I met the crew, and a darn good lot of chaps too:
Mr Rebel, Mr. Kennard, Mr. Harris, Mrs Brache, Ann, Noel,

No mattress, so had to sleep on straw for the night.

Well once more I sleep aboard the
"Reine D'Avor"
For how long I do not know, a good while I hope….

The Log of the Reine D'Avor

August 1938   **Wednesday 17**

Log of the "Reine D'Avor"

Slept like a log, straw not bad,
Seemed like (?) Ship steady as a rock,

Cancale a fine harbour,
Went ashore and got a new mattress
And pillow, it's made of dry seaweed,
Cost 80 francs, very cheap!
Got cigarettes, damn strong French ones
& a bit doubtful about new mattress,
will it stand damp sea air,
very nice one, smells good so far.

Mr. Kennard altered my bunk for me, made 6"
longer, he's a good carpenter,
I got my gear sorted out
somewhere near today,

We intend to sail in the morning I hope we do, we have a good ship and a darn good Crew, and we will get there this time…
Paid Brache…

The Log of the Reine D'Avor

August 1938　　　　　　　　**Thursday** 18

Left Cancale at 12 midday,
Fine weather,
Cow spit hit pier, very bad,

Used motor for 3 hrs,
Then carry on with sail,

Wind S. W., not a fair wind by a long way,
New mainsail not all it should be,

Work at 3hrs watches each,
I don't like it, I go on at
12 midday to 3 pm, every 12 hours.

Went on at midnight, nice breeze,
St Malo & Dinnard lights astern &
Cape Tell right abeam on Port,

Ship sailing herself, kept a look out
For the Rock Lowes light ahead,
But did not sight it,

The Log of the Reine D'Avor

August 1938 **Friday 19**

9.0 A.M.
had a good sleep, had some food, went on deck,
the wind was blowing a lot harder,
our course was dead into the wind,
so we had to keep tacking, damn hard work in a heavy sea,

12 midday went on watch, strong wind N.W. still tacking,
cross sea, very heavy, ship rolling all over the place,

1 P.M.
sighted Rock Lowes,

2 P.M.
wind blowing half a gale,
ship labouring very heavy,
very (?), took down big jib, put up small jib,
all of us have been sick, only Mr Rebel not sick.

The Log of the Reine D'Avor

August 1938   **Friday 19 cont.d**

2.30
Skipper changed course for Jersey,
lay up there for the night, raining,
visibility very bad, 1 mile,

Made Jersey **8.30 P.M**.
Miles from Cancale - about 70 all told,

Good old Jersey, never knew I would be here so soon...

The Log of the Reine D'Avor

August 1938 **Saturday 20**

Layed up in Jersey all day,
Went on shore, had darn good haircut and bath,
Wind still S.W.
Strong night wind had a good banging
Paid Skipper 2
Received 5£ from John,   car settled

August 1938 **Sunday 21**

Still tied up in Jersey. Wind still S.W. fair breeze
Worked on deck all day:
Oil tackle, fix new Main-throat sheet,
Glass rising,
fine weather ahead I hope,

Might go out tomorrow,
Wind gone round a bit.

The Log of the Reine D'Avor

August 1938 **Monday 22**

Still a wallflower in Jersey harbour.
Wind still SW x SSW, no good to us, Raining like the devil.

August 1938 **23/24 Tuesday**

Still a Wallflower in Jersey,Raining,
repair staysail this morning, Its done-for, and won't last us much longer; we are suppose to have a new one below;
the wind is going around a bit from W to N,
Glass rising,

The Log of the Reine D'Avor

August 1938   **Wednesday 25 (24?)**
                                                       (Day) 1

The "Reine D'Avor" sailed from Jersey at 5 P.M. 1hr after (?) bound for Las Palmas, Carn(ary) Islands.

Wind N.W., light air, Glass high,
Course W by N, sea smooth, speed 2 knots,

8.30 P.M.

sighted Rock Lowes Light,
log already 17 miles, when first part over,

Mr Lee joined ship today, if he only knew
what he was in for…
We are now ten people on the ship

The Log of the Reine D'Avor

August 1938   **Thursday (25)**
                                                                         (Day) 2

12 P.M. course S.E.
                           Log 93.
Wind light, sea rather big.

Ten people aboard, rather a crowd for a small ship like ours.

Five of us sailed the ship, the rest don't all work down below.

The Log of the Reine D'Avor

August 1938   **Friday (100)**
                                                    (Day) 3

9 A.M. course W by S   Log 20
12 A.M.   "   W by S   " 30
2.30 P.M. "   "   "   " 39

have now logged 120 miles

August 1938   **Saturday 27**
(Day) 4

12 P.M
Course S, Log 53
Wind N.S.W. light air. Sea calm,
Are now in steamship lane across the bay,
plenty of steamer,

will have (to) change tack soon,
or we will soon be in the bay.

The Log of the Reine D'Avor

August 1938 **Sunday 28 (200)**
                 (Day) 5

10 P.M.
Course S W   Log 70
Wind veering N to W, fair breeze,
Raining, sea moderate,

have now logged 253 miles from
Jersey, five day(s) out of Jersey,

Position about 40 mile W by S of Ushant
Just under ¼ of the way across the bay,
Have had to change tack twice,
Got a bang on the nose changing
Tack, from the big jib sheets,

12 A.M. noon
Wind rising N by W. strong breeze
Sea heavy, Log 75, small tear in staysail

                                            cont.d...

The Log of the Reine D'Avor

August 1938 **Sunday 28 (200)**
                          (Day5 cont.d)

8 P.M.

Wind very strong, N by W, just right, big seas,
Had to take down Missen, later down Forsail,

Two reefs in Mainsail, running now with
Reef mainsail & small jib, doing about 6 knots,
damn glad when we got through the Bay.

The Log of the Reine D'Avor

August 1938   **Monday 29   300
(Day) 6**

Went on watch at **12 A.M**. last night with George,
too strong wind & sea for one man

Wind very strong N by W course S by W.
Seas very big, still reefed down,
Sea coming aboard now & then,

Tony just about getting his sea legs,
Tony & Skipper came on at 3.30 A.M.

I felt like ten men at the end of that watch,
ten of them had, was I tired!

I slept from 4 A.M. to 11.30A.M.
The ship dancing all over the place,

The Log of the Reine D'Avor

August 1938   **Monday 29 300**
                                                      Day 6 cont

12 P.M.
noon - run 125

Wind going down still N by W, course S by W, Sea getting smaller, Sails still reefed,

Glass going up,
Noon Log 100, which meant it has been our best run as yet

from noon to noon 125 miles,
5 1/5 knots per hour for 24 hrs

have now logged 300 miles,
(position about 250, S W of **Ushant** –crossed through)

The Log of the Reine D'Avor

August 1938 **Tuesday 30**
 (Day) 7

8 A.M. No wind, sea small, Glass still
rising, ship rolling all over the place,

12 Noon.
No wind, sea big roll,
Log 55. 24 hrs run, - 55 miles.

1 P.M. Wind from S W course N by W,
light air, did 20 mile on this tack

5 P.M. calm then wind from N
course S W kept putting up and
taking down Main Sail,

8.30 School of Tunny fish around ship,
Tunny after small fish,
And kept jumping out of the sea
Noel had jammed up our tunny fishing gear as usual,
I put one line out,
but no luck,

18

The Log of the Reine D'Avor

August 1938   **Wednesday 31**
                                                     (Day) 8

---

12 A.M. Wind N of W, light air
ship hardly moving.
sea calm,

2.30 A.M. no wind, down main sail,
only jib and staysail up.

12 noon, still becalmed, lovely sunshine
log 86, run N to Noon 31 miles, glass high
position, about 200 mile across the bay.

12.30 P.M. Arthur, Tony & myself & Noel
went over the side, and had a good swim,
never thought I would swim
in the middle of the Bay of Biscay

position 2.30 P.M.
Latit 45.16 N   position 210 SW by S of Ushant
Longit 7.6 W
Log. 89

The Log of the Reine D'Avor

September 1938 **Thursday 1 429**
                    (Day) 9

12. Noon
Wind N E Course W by S
sea calm, log 45   noon 59, have now logged 429
Light air, tail wind, running free,

The best day we have had so far, as regards sunshine,
We did all intend to change our watches every week,
but today after a long talk they decided to leave their
watch as they were, bar Arthur & I, who changed, So
now I go on at 7.12 to 9.36 every 12 hours.
I get the chance of a decent sleep now at night,

I also have to get the breakfast, when possible,

I don't know how Arthur going to like my old watch
from 12 to 2.30, went on at 7.12 tonight and it now a
lovely evening,
the new moon was shining fine,
and the ship was running free,
she would not quite steer herself, just light wind, the
bay looked very nice for a change,

The Log of the Reine D'Avor

September 1938 **Friday 2   538**
                                        (Day) 10

12 Noon

Wind N E, strong breeze,
sea fairly heavy, Glass light steady.
Log 38. Course W by S.   Max speed 6 knots
Noon run 983,

Have now logged 538 miles from Jersey, I think

We are somewhere about 180 miles N W of Finisterre,

Well out of the Bay...   cont.d ...

The Log of the Reine D'Avor

September 1938   **Friday 2   538**
                                                  (Day) 10 cont

---

**It came on to blow harder early this morning.
I wake up at 7 A.M. to hear plenty of rain on deck,**

I went up and Mr. Rebell, Arthur, George, were reefing up the Mainsail,

**The jib tackle for jib stay and half-yard had carried away,
the big jib of course went over the bow with it,**

George was on watch, he left the big jib up too long, we darn lucky it did not carry the top of the mast away with it, it will one of these days, so now we are running free with our Mainsail well reefed down and Staysail, no Missen, and we can't use our jib yet, somebody still have to go up the mast and free it…** (see page 24)

September 1938 **Friday 2 (cont)**

6 P.M.
Wind N E fair breezes tail W
Sea heavy, Glass 30.5, Course W by S
Position 44.15   Lat N
13.19   Lon W
200 miles N W of Finisterre

8.30 P.M.
changed Course to S by ½ W. log. 71.
Wind N.E fair going down, tail W.
Sea big swell, Glass 30.5,
Took down Staysail which had torn badly,
Put jib on staysail haliyard,

The Log of the Reine D'Avor

September 1938   **Saturday 3 10**
                                                           (Day) 11

12 Noon

Wind S E light. Course S.
sea calm, Glass 30.6
log 10
Noon run 72.

2.30 P.M.

**
Arthur went up the top of the
Mast and fixed a new block for the jib haliyard.
We got the jib up soon afterwards.

The Log of the Reine D'Avor

September 1938 **Sunday 4 710**
                                        (Day) 12

12 Noon Wind S E   Course S W
sea choppy Glass 30.5
Log 10 Noon run 100

Position about 200 miles W of Vigo, Spain,

I have not seen a ship for 4 days, our true course now is S.
So we have all hope for wind anywhere near N.

Mr Rebell put on another patch on the Staysail,
it will soon be all patches, damned old sail,
our big balloon jib is a fine sail, but got a big bag in it, and it not much good for close hauling,
it's a fine sail for running free,
one of these days it will be left up too long in a stiff wind, and it will be carried away & our top mast with it,
George has nearly managed it.
6.45 P.M.   Log 30
Lat   42.11 N
Long   15.11 W   285 W of Vigo.

The Log of the Reine D'Avor

September 1938 **Monday 5 810**
                                              (Day) 13

---

12 Noon   Wind E, fair breeze, Course S
Sea choppy,   Glass 30.6
Log 10
Noon run 100.   Av speed 4 knts.

('Our longitude is now' – crossed through)...

We are now true North of
Las Palmas.   Lon 15o (degrees) W
Position   Lon 14.51 W
Lat 40.15 N

Somewhere West between Opporto & Lisbon

4.30 P.M.

sighted big steamer going W,
most likely out of Lisbon,
first steamer we have see(n) for 5 days.

The Log of the Reine D'Avor

September 1938   **Tuesday 6 918**
(Day) 14

---

12 Noon, Wind NNE, Course S.
Sea choppy swell   Glass 30.5   Log 18
Noon run 108   Sp 4½ knots

2.30 A.M. during Authur watch, the big jib sheet broke,
I woke up to hear a banging and smashing of sails, up I go to find Arthur, Tony and Mr. Rebell getting the jib in,
just as we got the darn sail in, there was a bang up aloft, and away goes the throat haliyards on the Mainsail,
down comes the Mainsail ½ way,

The peach haliyard had all the weight, we certainly jump to it, and got it down damn quick,
so we let her sail the rest of the night on Missen, Staysail & small jib, we are running free, so it not bad, she still doing the knots
I wonder how Tony would have got on if he had been on watch alone!
10 A.M. stick up the big jib, spliced the sheet,
and the Main throat haliyard.

The Log of the Reine D'Avor

September 1938 **Wednesday 7   1010**
                    (Day) 15

---

12 Noon. Wind NNE Course S.
Sea choppy. Glass 30.5. Log 10.
Noon run 92.

More trouble with the big jib again during Skipper's watch,
the jib hoist, and stud bill rope hoisted;
out and down into the sea goes the jib, a damn fine game gathering it in again, so we are now running free with only Missen and staysail, they keep jibbing, so we had to spend most of today making repairs,

position 7 P.M.   Log 24
Latit 37o (degrees)   22 N
Long   W. 14o (degrees) 14

We are approx 550 miles N of Las Palmas
Mr. Rebell shows me the working out of
today positions Lat & Long. I thought there
was a lot in it, now I am darn sure of it.

I shaved today, first time since leaving
Jersey, it's worth it.

September 1938   **Thursday 8 1110**
                                                   (Day) 16

12 Noon
Wind N W moderate breeze
Course SSW, Sea choppy, Glass 30.5
Log 9

Roon run 100   Spd 4 & $1/6^{th}$ knots.
running free, Main stay & jib,

Wind went round from NNE to NW at 5 A.M.,
Course then S,
changed course at 7 A.M. to SSW

Log then 81
Lati noon 36o (degrees) 18 W   Log 9 12
Noon

Position 6 P.M.   Log 31
Latit   35.58   N
Longit 13.45   W

The Log of the Reine D'Avor

September 1938   **Friday 9 1222**
                                                    (Day) 17

---

12 Noon
breeze, Course S.
Sea heavy.
Log 31
noon run 122

Wind   NNE,   fair

Glass 30.5 Tem(p) 71

Speed 5 & $1/12^{th}$

We are running free, with big blue seas following us astern, and with the sun shining well, it's the sort of day that I like at sea; the ship is hard to steer like this; a big sea hit her on her quarter, and throws her bow right(s) off some times to port, and sometimes to starboard,

when she goes to starboard then its 'look out', you have to get her back on her course before another sea get you, that's where she would jib, and the 'boom' like a gun when it does come over,
still, we have luckily, we have not had a bad jib yet, and with the fair winds we are having, we won't be long before we arrive off Las Palmas.

6.30   Log 66
        Latit 33o (degrees)   53 N
        Long 13o (degrees)   11 W

The Log of the Reine D'Avor

September 1938   **Saturday 10**
                                                            (Day) 18

12 A.M. [Midnight]
I took over my old watch back from Arthur, relieving Mr. Rebell.

The wind was a strong breeze on the quarter, and the following seas were very big breakers, which threw the ship either way off her course, so it was careful work at the helm,

Well I had been at the helm for about 1½ hrs when the wind started to blow harder, and now and then into violent squalls, then I got the biggest seas that we had this trip.

You always seem to get these very big rollers following each other. After a time, seas wanted to drive over the stern; the ship was doing about 8 and over. The wind and seas got too bad. The ship seemed to be carried along on the top of the rollers, sometimes it seemed faster than the seas ('of the wing' – crossed through) then she seemed to lose steering away, and I had a hell of a job to hold her on her course. cont.d...

The Log of the Reine D'Avor

September 1938 **Saturday 10**
Day 18 cont.d

cont...

I knew then it was time to reef sail. I called out to the skipper, he came up, half asleep, he darn soon woke up, he called up all hands, and we soon reefed her down.

Tony was one of the first up on deck. I don't think he ever sleeps in a blow.

When I put the ship about into the wind for reefing, she went head to sea of course, then we got the seas aboard, we down stay and well-reefed the missen,
... no missen, put her back on her course again, and the skipper and Tony stay on watch, it was time for his watch, I was glad to get to sleep.

cont/d ...(new page)...

The Log of the Reine D'Avor

September 1938   **Saturday 10 cont/d**

cont...

She made a new record run, from 12 midnight last night to 12 tonight, of 136 miles, speed 5½, her best noon-to-noon
run being   125   "   , speed 5 & 1/5th

12 noon Wind NNE strong breeze
Course S
sea big rollers, Glass 30.5, Tem(p) 71   Log 60
noon run 129, speed 5 & 1/3rd (best time as yet)
log 63

noon Latitude 32o (degrees) 15 N   180 Miles N of Lanzarote

Position 7 P.M. Log 92
Latitude 31o (degrees) 44 N
Longitude, 12o (degrees) 38 W

The Log of the Reine D'Avor

September 1938   **Sunday 11   1471**
                                        (Day) 19

12 Noon

Wind NNE, fair breeze, Course S x E
sea small rollers, Glass 30.4,   Tem(p) 71.5,   Log 71
noon run 111, speed 4 & 1/3rd
Noon Latit 30o (degrees) 41 N, which I worked out for the first time correct, thanks to Mr. Rebell.

6.30 P.M.
Latit 30.20   Long 11.48
Log 98 about 100 miles NE of the most Ely Island, should see it tomorrow.

34

The Log of the Reine D'Avor

September 1938   **Monday 12   1587**
                                    (Day) 20

12 A.M. midnight,
Wind N by E, light air, Course W by S,
sea calm, spd 3 knots. We should be quite near one of the Islands now, but did not see any lights during my watch.

6 A.M.
Island sighted right from Bearing, leeward, Island bearing S, we should clear on this course.
Island name Allegeanya (Allegany?)

12 Noon
Wind light, air NNE, Course W by S,
sea calm, Glass 30.4, Tem 71, Log 87
Noon run 117, Spd 5k. Noon latit 29.39, which I worked out.

1 P.M. cleared Allegeanya (Allegany?), and sighted Lanzarote and faintly Fuenteventura.

The Log of the Reine D'Avor

September 1938 **Tuesday 13 167 (Day) 21**

12 Noon,

Wind NE, light air, Course W by S, sea calm,
spd. 2 knots, Glass 30.4, Tem 71, Log 74,
noon run 87 mile,

5 P.M.
sighted Las Palmas, bearing SW by S,
we are well to N, windward of it, the wind is very light, will not be able to make it today, so will close up, and tack around all night.

6.30 P.M. sighted the Peak of Tenerife, bearing W, very high in the sky.

Closed up on light house on headland near harbour,
And tack up and down all night.

The Log of the Reine D'Avor

September 1938   **Wednesday 14 1714**
                              (Day) 22

8 A.M. on tack back to headland,
Las Palmas harbour just the other side.

12 Noon, Wind light NNE, Sea calm, Log 14, noon run 40, are now bearing in to Las Palmas bay,

Pick up Pilot, enter harbour and
Anchored at 3 P.M.
Total Miles 1714,   22 days Total.

The Island is under Martial law, under General Franco's Rebel Government, we had a soldier & sailor guard put aboard directly we got in harbour, and nobody could go ashore except the skipper, we have got to get a pass first, too too bad for us.

The seamen Mission sent us some fruit, it did not last long,
A troopship left here tonight full, for Franco's army.

37

The Log of the Reine D'Avor

September 1938 **Thursday 15**

I had a darn good sleep, strange the ship as steady as a rock.

The guard has to stay on board night and day, they have a tug on guard at the harbour mouth all night, we could not leave harbour without them knowing

I going ashore tomorrow with the boys, with a pass, after tomorrow we won't need passes,

Las Palmas harbour is a very big one. We have got the agent of **the Elder Demster shipping line** looking after us, very good chap.

The Island Princess, a liner, came in this afternoon.

The Log of the Reine D'Avor

September 1938　　　　　　　　**Thursday 15
cont.d**

There is fine boat here from Norway, the
"Osgar Tybring", she has, being a lifeboat, about 40 ton, Cutter rig, she is on a World cruise, 3 chaps, her next port is Barbados.

The Log of the Reine D'Avor

September 1938   **Friday 16**

Went ashore at **Las Los, Las Palmas** for the first time,
the town is not quite what I expected, but its pretty good,

Arthur, George, and I had a darn good walk through and round it, went to Seamen Mission, and found G.P.O.

found out that all letters are censored, got to be careful what I write in my letters,

Plenty of soldiers about and War Writers, the girls are all dark, true Spanish, they don't give the glad eye, have not got them weighed up at all!

We walk all day, walk to town in the morning, and walk our feet off coming back in the evening, legs very tired, darn glad to get to sleep.

September 1938 Saturday 17

Got up about 7, darn tired, felt rotten all day,
Wrote a few letters to catch

Mail Boat Rochester Castle, leaving early Sunday morning for England, 4½ days trip, sure is going some,

(Sunday 18 – Thursday 22 September 1938 no diary entries)

The Log of the Reine D'Avor

September 1938   **Friday 23**

Went to pictures at **Las Los**, some darn place, people only go once, worst one I have been to, they can't smoke inside, went from there to Mission, people there very nice,

We heard the Wireless news from London, things are getting very bad.

The Log of the Reine D'Avor

September 1938 **Saturday 24**

Tony and I intended to go up country to
Monte. this morning, got to town, find bus too crowded, too bad,
next bus 1½ hrs later, so thought better of it,

So, we (are) some place up in the hills called **Bridgcar (Brigida?),** long ride, some bus, not much to see, see camel on its last legs, the hills are very dry, everything burnt up, not worth seeing.

We had an invitation from **P Demster**, who is the Island agent for all English ships, to get to Island Yacht club dance tonight in honour of the
Cunard Liner visit, the Lanchastrian(?)

The Liner is on a 12-day tour, came in this morn,
Mrs Brache, Ann, Tony, I went, the other(s) backed out,
It was a good dance, **Mr. Demster** parked us with a crowd off the liner, just right, got to know a very nice Cornwall, Penzance girl, dance finish at 1,   Girl would like to come on our trip, wish she could, she had to get back to Liner, it sailed at 3 A.M. for Tenerife, too, too bad,

The Log of the Reine D'Avor

September 1938   **Sunday 25**

Tony and I went for a swim this morning at the **Hotel Metropole**, very good Lido, had the best swim for weeks, the charge at 2½ Pesetas = 11 ½ d, darn robbers,
One Peseta = about 4 ½ d = approx 53 to the Pound,

Their money values go as Peseta paper money,
Peseta divides into Cents, Penny & halfpennies,
One penny = 10 Cents,   1/10th of a Peseta
Halfpenny = 5 Cents =   1/20th " " Peseta
Also 25 Cents prices.

I think had enough of this place, Be glad to get to sea again. **The Metropole Hotel** being the English Hotel for the Island, I thought we might be lucky this morning, but no go, did not meet any English people at all, German Yacht came in late last night
Name, 'Arga', about 30 ton, white Schooner rig, fine fast boat, in the afternoon Mr. Rebell and I spoke to them,
Mr. Rebell speaks German, **'Arga'** fishing between Islands,

The Log of the Reine D'Avor

September 1938   **Monday** 26

Arthur complained of pains in his stomach and a bad headache last night, he had a high temperature 101o (degrees), darned if I know what was wrong. I put him to bed on the deck.
He been in the sun too much.

This morning Arthur worse, gave him two aspirins, Temp still high, sick, & pain in neck & stomach, could not keep still in bed, too much pain.
He got very bad towards evenings,
Got a doctor for him, Doc was Spanish, but could speak French.
He said Arthur had got a local fever, and a very bad chill; gave me two very big Pills to give him, also Epsom Salts, gave him one pill tonight, had to get up during night, Arthur nearly helpless.

The Log of the Reine D'Avor

September 1938 **Tuesday 27**

Arthur lay in bed, can hardly speak, no sleep, Temp lower, bad pain stomach, can't hold anything, wish we could get him to Hospital ashore, no place for him on this ship, they make too much damn noise, gave him some Epsom salts this morning.

The Log of the Reine D'Avor

September 1938   **Wednesday 28**

Arthur no better this morning.
no sleep at all last night, that's two nights without no sleep, cannot eat, when he drinks pain in stomach, then up it comes, within ten minutes,
he was in very bad pain again this afternoon.

I'll have to get him sleeping powder of some sort,
got doctor about sleeping powder,
he gave me eight very small ones, containing Opium, to be taken one only when he's in great pain, also a bottle of something to inject into him, four injections all told, one night & morning, poor old Arthur, he ought to be ashore in Hospital.

Well I gave him his first injections late tonight.
George and I gave him one sleeping Pill.
he was very quiet during night,

The Log of the Reine D'Avor

September 1938 **Thursday 29**

Arthur better today.
gave him injections, wash him,
changed his sheets,

The Log of the Reine D'Avor

September 1938 **Friday 30**

Gave Arthur his last injection this morning,
no change for yesterday, he did not sleep
much last night,

I cleaned the deck down today,
The dirty 'B.B's I don't think she had decent clean for a Yr.

It took me all darn day, it was a different ship when I finished. There is so much junk on deck, you don't know what to do with it, only one way that I know, that is throw it overboard.

The Log of the Reine D'Avor

October 1938 **Saturday 1**

Arthur a little better today, made a bed for him on deck,
he was up there all day, he is still very weak,

Today ashore is **Franco's show day**, every ship in the harbour is dressed, I did what I could with our six flags!
They had a soldier & sailor review on one part of the harbour, too far away for us to see much,

The Log of the Reine D'Avor

October 1938 — Sunday 2

Arthur much better, he will soon be O.K.

(Monday 3 – Wednesday 5 October, 1938, no diary entries)

The Log of the Reine D'Avor

October 1938 **Thursday 6**

Today we move the ship over to a small beach in the harbour on the flood, and at low water, cleaned or tried to clean her bottom,
We manage it after two days, then move out into the harbour again,

(Friday 7 – Sunday 9 October, 1938, no diary entries)

October 1938   Monday 10

Tony & Arthur had a few words this morning, over nothing

Tony went over to the **"Osgar Tybring"** and told them the tale, and he joined them,

They took him, for how long I don't know,

Well, that is that, Tony finished with the "Reine D'Avor",

(Tuesday 11 - Wednesday 12 October, 1938, no diary entries)

The Log of the Reine D'Avor

October 1938　　　　　　　　　　**Thursday 13**

Big Bill paid today, by Arthur & George,
some stores came aboard today,
thank the Lord that Bill is paid,

The agent **Elder Demster** nothing but
a darn robber,

The Log of the Reine D'Avor

October 1938 **Friday 14**
`(31)

Last stores came aboard this morning,
We intend to Sail at dawn tomorrow,
"Osgar Tybring" also sailing tomorrow.

Sid in Harbour…

The Log of the Reine D'Avor

October 1938   **Saturday 15**
                                                (Set Sail – Day) 1

Sailed from Las Palmas at **3.15 P.M**. local time
Wind light. N. Sea calm.

All-wayed, all-paid, now for Barbados.

"Osgar Tybring" sailed at **2 P.M**.

The Skipper & Arthur had another go today,
I think Barbados will be the end of this trip,

it too too bad, but we can't keep on like this,
Skipper said he was going to sail out of Harbour,
same old damn game, we had a fair wind,
then he could not do it, engine, darn engine,

Well, after being 31 days in Grand Canary at last
we leave it, 31 days too much,
Good bye and blow yer, nothing but trouble there,

Position **La Lus Harbour**
Latit   28.8   N
Lon   15.26   W
10 P.M. have sailed in line with **Grand Can**
about 8 miles off **La Lus E.**

The Log of the Reine D'Avor

The Osgar Tybring – in full sail

The Log of the Reine D'Avor

October 1938 **Sunday 16 30**
                  (Day) 2

12 Months ago today we left Jersey on the same trip,
I was damn lucky to get back there again,
Where we will end this time, Lord knows

We changed our watches one ahead, I go on now at 2.24 to 4.48 every 12 hrs,

I going to be Cook for midday dinner between here & Barbados, that is if they can stand it that long. I'll make them sleep all right. Dinner today, lettuce, Toms, Potatoes, fresh fish, carrots,

12 Noon, Wind light NE, Course S, Log. 30
our speed about 3 knts, we are sailing well away from the Land before we head to S. Westward
Skipper frightened of getting in Lee of Grand Canary, says there 25 miles of Calm Leeward of it, nuts,
The "Osgar Tybring" just sailed away from us, cannot see anything of her today, don't expect to see them until we get to port

We are about 20 miles S.S.E. of the Island

The Log of the Reine D'Avor

October 1938   **Monday 17 86**
                                                (Day) 3

---

12 Noon   Wind light NE, Course W by S
Log. 86
Glass 34.7   Tem(p) 77.   Sea small,
noon run 56   Trade wind not so good,
We are running free now with our big Spinnaker, first time we have used it abeam, I think our Spd about 4 knts.

I had a sudden rain squall on my watch early this morning, rain heavy for about five minutes.

Arthur gets a bad cold, can't do his watch today,
Alter all our Watches again to cover Arthur's,
I do 9 to 12, a 3 hr watch

The Log of the Reine D'Avor

October 1938	**Tuesday 18 208**
	(Day) 4

12 Noon   Wind fair breeze N by E Course W S W
Sea small, Glass 34.2, Tem 78, Log 8
noon run, 122   speed 5 knots,
our Spinnaker is pulling fine,

Arthur still unwell,

5 P.M. took down Spinnaker, and put it up on Cowspit as balloon jib, it's a very big Sail, and might be too bad if we got caught in a bad squall at night with it, it is our old Bermudian Mainsail,

The Log of the Reine D'Avor

October 1938 **Wednesday 19 338**
                                    (Day) 5

---

12 Noon, Wind fair Breeze N by E, Course W S W Sea small, Glass 34.3, Tem(p) 78, Log 38 noon run 130,   spd. 5½ knts.

Arthur still unwell; I think it really the result of a bad cold again,
Sighted Steamer heading NE, I think it's the last one we shall see for a long time.
Mrs. B had a go at me today, the 'B.B'.!
sighted plenty of lightning last night bearing N during my watch, Mr. Rev follows me on watch at 12 Midnight, he was quite unconcerned about the lightning, I did not like it so good, it missed us, but Reb does not worry much,

I'm still Cook, I'll make them all sick yet,

The Log of the Reine D'Avor

October 1938　　　　**Thursday 20 468**
　　　　　　　　　　　　　　　(Day) 6

12 Noon. Wind N E, Course W S W
Sea bit choppy, Glass 34.6, Tem 79, Log. 68
noon run 130 M. Spd 5½ knts.
Arthur a bit better today, still not fit for work during my watch last night, our first flying fish came aboard, he hit the stern of our punt; he fell on the deck, 2ft away from me at the helm, made me jump!
he was about 10" long, I cooked him for Arthur's dinner today, hope we get some more tonight

The Log of the Reine D'Avor

October 1938   **Friday 21 Record run**
     611   **(Day) 7**

12 Noon   Wind NE, Course W S W
Sea heavy, Glass 34.7, Tem 78, Log 11
Noon run 143 Miles, Spd 6 knots,

Today's run is a new record, the fastest time the ship has made for 24 hrs,
Trade wind this last 24 hrs & steady fast breeze, about 22 M.P.H,
We are covering the miles all right; still we have got a long way to go,

Did not get any flying fish last night,
Arthur a lot better today,

I have moved up to cooking breakfast now, instead of dinner, George is the best Cook on the ship, so therefore George will do his stuff on the dinner…Good Old George!

The Log of the Reine D'Avor

October 1938   **Saturday 22   Record run**
    756   **(Day) 8**

12 Noon, Wind NE fair breeze, Course W by S, Sea heavy, Glass 34.5, Tem 79, Log. 56
Noon run 145 M,   Spd 6 & 1/24th kts.
today run another new record, two miles faster

2.30 A.M. during Mr. Reb's watch the big balloon jib carried away, there was not much wind at the time. The sail is split from top to bottom; past repair, we will have to make a small jib out of what's left of it,

10 A.M. during my watch, I saw plenty of flying fish; they seem to be always getting out of the boat's way,

Arthur seems a lot better today,

The Log of the Reine D'Avor

| **October 1938** | **Sunday 23**
(Day) 9 | **890** |

12 Noon Wind N E Light breeze, Course W by S, Heavy Choppy Sea, B. 33.4, T. 79o (degrees), Log 90 run 134, Spd 5 & $7/12^{th}$ knots

The Trade wind shows a tendency to moderate at night time
We have our Mainsail, small jib & Staysail up now, the Missen not much good to us,

The Log of the Reine D'Avor

October 1938 **Monday 24 1010**
 (Day) 10

Noon Wind E by N Light breeze, Course S W Choppy Sea, Glass. B. 30.33, Tem(p) 80, Log. 10 run, 120, Spd 5 knots

Put Ship Clock back one hr today.

The Log of the Reine D'Avor

October 1938   **Tuesday 25**
1119   **(Day) 11**

Noon Wind E by N Light breeze, Course W S W, Sea going down, B. 30.3, T. 80, Log. 19 run 109, 4½ knots.

3 P.M.
The Wind being light, took down small jib, put up Spinnaker which draws well,

Arthur came back on his watch today, after being off sick for nine day: he had a very bad cold; I get to go back to my 2.24 to 4.48 Watch now, rotten watch,

9 P.M. Mrs. 'B.B'. had a go at me again, (darn),

The Log of the Reine D'Avor

October 1938   **Wednesday 26**
1225   **(Day) 12**

Noon Wind E by N fair breeze, Course W S W
Sea small, B 30.23, T. 80, Log. 25
run 106, spd 4½ k,

Our position now is about half way across,
that's only dead reckoning and + drift Ocean Currents
about ½ knot per day E,
allow 150 miles on 12 days run 1225 + 150 = 1375
across

The Log of the Reine D'Avor

October 1938   **Thursday 27 1338**
                                                   (Day) 13

Noon Wind E by N light, Course W S W
Sea small, B. 30.31, T. 80½ (degrees), Log. 38
run 113, Spd 4½ knts.

very hot today,
B drives us nuts with her book reading. B,
Useless her one and only name,

12 A.M. Steamer, a big oil tanker, sighted, heading N W, first ship we've seen for eight days.

The Log of the Reine D'Avor

October 1938   **Friday 28**
1452   **(Day) 14**

Noon Wind E light breeze, Course W by S, Sea small B. 30.3, T. 80½ (degrees), Log. 52 run 114, Spd 4½ knts.

5 P.M. Local Time, Log. 14.74.
Latit   13.17.N, which is nearly the Latit of Barbados, which means we are really too far south, we have about another 1000 miles to go, Well we have to sail true West if possible.

Today's Lonti not certain 35.50 W, position just over half way across, 1440 miles sailed, 1380 miles to go,

The Log of the Reine D'Avor

October 1938 **Saturday 29 1566**
 (Day) 15

11.30 A.M.
　　Changed course to True W, Log. 64,
　　Noon Wind Light E, Cour(se) True W.
　　Sea small. B. 30.24, T. 81, Log. 66
　　Run 114m, spd 4½ knt.

The Log of the Reine D'Avor

October 1938 **Sunday 30 1677**
                          (Day) 16

Noon Wind N by E light breeze. Cour(se) True W,
Sea small chop, B. 30.3, T. 81, Log. 77,
run 111, Spd 4½ knts.

12 noon I worked out Latit 12o(degrees) N.
Barbados lays on Latit 13o (degrees), difference just
over 60 miles to the South the Islands parallel,
S obs 9ft 64.07, Solar Noon, G.M.T. 2.25 = 14.25
Log. 77. the Latit. 12o (degrees) N

If wind veers any more to North, we will have to
down Spinnaker, and put it up on the Cowspit,
We have been very lucky with this crossing so far,
every day since leaving Las Palmas we have had sunny Weather, and a nice soft breeze, the Trade wind
lives up to it(s) name,

The Log of the Reine D'Avor

October 1938 **Monday 31 1770**
                  (Day) 17

Noon Wind N by E. light Air, Cou(rse) True W.
Sea Calm, B. 30.33, T. 81, Log. 70
run 93. Spd 4 knts.

The Log of the Reine D'Avor

November 1938 **Tuesday 1 1870**
                  (Day) 18

Noon Wind E. light. Cour(se) W by N True.
Sea calm. B. 30.33, T. 81, Log. 70
run 100, Spd 4 & 1/6th knts.

Noon Wind very light, boom banging about, bash, bang,
Weather fine, Sun darn hot.

6 P.M. position Latit   12o(degrees).09
Long 42o(" ").49

I worked out Latit. and after a hell of a job worked out the
Long.,

The Log of the Reine D'Avor

November 1938   **Wednesday 21962
(Day) 19**

Noon Wind E. light, Course W by N True.
Sea Calm. B. 30.4, T. 81, Log. 62
run 92. Spd 4 knts Wind right astern

1 P.M. boom banging too much, Wind right astern, sea rotten roll, put Guys on Main Boom & Pack up forward, let Main S(sail) right out, lot better,

4 P.M. had rain squalls, took spinnaker up small jib

The Log of the Reine D'Avor

November 1938 **Thursday 3 2074**
 (Day) 20

Noon Wind E fair breeze, Course. W by N True.
Sea Choppy, B. 30.4, T. 81½ (degrees), Log. 74
run 112, spd. 4½ knts.

10 A.M. down jib, up Spinnaker, Mainsail squared,

8 P.M. Position Latit   12o(degrees).53 N.
Long 46o(degrees).17 W.
Which I worked out, passed by the mate, Log 2094.
Leaving us 780 miles East of Barbados. 8 days sail
and I hope we will be there,

The Log of the Reine D'Avor

November 1938   **Friday 4 2194**
                              (Day) 21

Noon Wind E by N fair breeze, Course W True
Sea Choppy. B.   T.   Log. 94
run 120, spd 5 knts.

4 P.M.   Latit   13.09 N
Long 48o(degrees) 46 W
about 600 miles to go,
"   3 hrs difference with G.M.T. and our Ship time.

The Log of the Reine D'Avor

November 1938 **Saturday 5 320**
                   (Day) 22

Noon Wind E by N fair breeze, W True
Sea choppy, B. 30.23, T. 80½, Log. 20
run 126, Spd 5 knts.

These days are lovely Sailing days, nice soft fair winds, lovely sunshine, it great to be at sea in this weather,

These morning(s), during my watch from 2.30 A.M. to 4.48, I can still see the North star very clear, it fairly low in the sky,

The Log of the Reine D'Avor

November 1038   **Sunday 6 2463**
                              (Day) 23

Noon Wind E. Strong breeze, Course W. Mag.
Sea, heavy chop. B. 30.23,   T. 82,   Log 63
run, 143,   Spd 6 knots.

noon position   Latit 13o (degrees) 2N.
fine breeze, old "Reine" doing her stuff,
six knots, she would make a fine photo now, with her
Main and Spin right out, and a big following sea,

Ship time 5 P.M. Long. 53o (degrees) 30W.
position 360 Miles True East of Barbados

1 P.M. laceing on Gaff broke, it was down Spinnaker, down Mainsail, up with Stay & jib.
lucky it broke during day-time,
re-lace sail on Gaff and up she went, now running under Main Stay & jib, alter course to W by N. true, Wind is veering E to N, sea rising, too big a roll for Spinnaker, doing about 5½ knots.

The Log of the Reine D'Avor

November 1938   **Monday 7**
2570   **(Day) 24**

Noon. Wind E fair breeze, Course W by N, Sea big swell. B. 30.23. T. 81. Log 70 run 107. 4½ knts.

Noon   Latit 13.26 N.

11 P.M. Last night, the Log carried away off the end of its line, replace with new Log at 12 noon today

1 P.M. down Jib, up Spinnaker and alter course to True West, as our noon Latit is in line with North end of the Island, Bridgetown the harbour is South end of it,

5 P.M. Long 55o (degrees) 25, 230 miles to go, my Long was 55o (degrees) 18, 7 miles out.

9 P.M. had a good view of the Moon's Eclipse tonight.

The Log of the Reine D'Avor

November 1938   **Tuesday 8 2710**
                                (Day) 25

Noon. Wind E. Strong breeze. Course W. True
Sea very heavy. B. 30.23.   T. 81.   Log 10
run 140. app 6 knts.
five miles short of record run,

3.30 A.M. during my watch the StaySail sheet parted, I could not leave helm, Mate fix it, the heaviest running sea for a long time,
Noon latit 13o (degrees) 32 N, about 120 miles to go, we are a little too much to the North.

5 P.M. Long 57o (degrees) 47 W.
about 105 miles East of Island.
3 P.M. mate wanted to alter course to S. run down about 30 miles as our Latit was too much to the North also current taking us N W.

Skipper looked to the South, see a dark cloud there, it frightened him, he said "no", we turn south tomorrow.
Mate told him he never 'ort to have gone to sea, Mate said we might pass the Island if don't run South, we did not.

The Log of the Reine D'Avor

November 1938 **Wednesday 9 2832**
                   (Day) 26

Wind N E strong breeze. Course. W. True.
Sea heavy swell. B. 30.02. T. 81. Log 32
run 122 Spd. 5 knts

Noon Latit 13o (degrees) 45 N, just 44 miles out of our course, lovely helmsmen we have.

1 P.M. Alter course to S W Mag log. 39
Strong squalls plenty of rain,
we (are) still have one reef in Mainsail.

10 P.M. sighted Steamer Cargo, bound S. W.
first ship we have seen for 14 days,

3 P.M. still very squally, rain heavy, can see no more than about 1 mile at time.

3.30   Mate cannot get sight, no sun, thinks we have miss(ed) Island, and so do I, he hoved-ship-to all night,
What a skipper we have got,

The Log of the Reine D'Avor

November 1938   **Thursday 1 2880**
                                    (Day) 27

Wind E fair breeze.   Course S E Mag.
Sea heavy swell. B. 30.22.   T. 81.   Log.80
run 48 miles.

noon Latit 13.20 N   )
7 A.M. Long. 60o (degrees) 7 W   ) ?

7 A.M. sighted two Islands, from bearing taking they are St. Vincent bearing W., St. Lucia bearing N W, which means that we have passed Barbados all right, we missed it in the rain yesterday, if we had only gone south when the Mate wanted us, we would have made the Island all right.

Well, here we are now in the Lee, halfway Barbados and St. Vincent,

We shall have to tack all the way back there,
The ship sails herself, quite a change,

The Log of the Reine D'Avor

November 1938 **Friday 11 929**
                                         (Day) 28

Wind light air. E.   Course E of N.
Sea calm.   B. 30.23.   T. 82½. Log. 29
run 49 miles.

noon Latit 12.40. N.
still tacking back to Barbados,
have change(d) tack 3 times, on a port tack now,
the Current here is about 1½ knots a day against us.
it sets N W.

7.16 P.M.
Long. 60o (degrees).11

The Log of the Reine D'Avor

November 1938 **Saturday 12 2977 (Day) 29**

Wind, light E.   Course N N E, star(board) tack
Sea calm.   B. 30.33.   T. 82. Log. 77
run 28 miles

change tack twice during night,
speed about 1½ knots.
Noon Latit 13.18.N

2 P.M. changed over to P(port) tack,
wind very light, hardly any way.

The Log of the Reine D'Avor

November 1938   **Sunday 13 3009**
                              (Day) 30

Wind. Light Air. E.   Course E of N. P(port) tack
Sea Calm,   B. 30.33.   T.   82½,
     Log 9   run 32.

Still tacking N then S. can't make much Easting at all, it's a game of patience, the Skipper doesn't seem too worried, I don't think he wants to make Barbados,

The Log of the Reine D'Avor

November 1938	**Monday 14 3052 (Day) 31**

Wind fair N E.　　Course S E.　　S(starboard) tack
Sea calm,　　　　B. 30.33.　　　T. 81½o (degrees).
　　　Log 52
run 43 miles

11 P.M. Sighted Island bearing East, abeam of us, also steamer making for it,
Island must be 35 miles away,
just make it out, hope we keep it in sight, doubt it,

Staysail tore up during Arthur watch last night,replace with another old Staysail at 10 A.M., the old sail not done bad, lasted for 4800 miles, this one is a bit bigger than the old one,

Well roll up Barbados, this is the six(th) day()s we been trying to get back,

87

The Log of the Reine D'Avor

November 1938   **Tuesday 15 120**
                     (Day) 32

Wind fair N E.   Course S E.   St(starboard) tack
Sea Calm,   B. 30.3 T 81½ Log. 20
run 68

Sighted Barbados at 9 A.M., abeam to Eastward, about 30 miles off, very Low,

Noon Latit 13o (degrees).5 N

had one bad squall during night,
drop Stay & Missen darn quick, it soon blew itself out

The Log of the Reine D'Avor

November 1938   **Wednesday 16 3170**
                          (Day) 33

Wind light S E.   Course E.
    Port tack
Sea calm,   B. 30.3, T 82,   Log. 70
run 50,

10 A.M. sighted Barbados dead ahead,
if wind holds will make it,

11 A.M. Wind very squally, plenty of rain, Island disappeared in the rain, Wind setting in now from S E,

12 (noon) Island nearer, are now passing small fishing boats, 3 miles off Island,
Wind kind to us, heading in right for harbour,

4.30 P.M. in harbour, after sailing 3170 miles,
32 days at sea,   **cont.d...**

The Log of the Reine D'Avor

November 1938   **Wednesday 16 3170
(Day) 33 contd**

cont.

"Osgar Tybring" arrive here eight days ago, we ought to have beaten them, "Osgar's" Skipper & Mate came aboard as soon as we arrived, we cleared Customs; then "Osgar's" Skipper took us to a good anchorage, he's a very decent chap, they gave us tea aboard "Osgar" yacht good

Osgar Tybring – [print version]

The Log of the Reine D'Avor

November 1938 **Thursday 17**

The old ship very steady again, had a nice long sleep for a change,

8.30 A.M.
local chaps all around ship, wanting work of all descriptions,

Arthur and I went for a real good swim to the beach, it was about 300 yards all told; the swim was great, one of the best I have ever had, the water like warm milk,
My mail arrive OK,

3.30 P.M.
A and I went ashore, and we are very please(d) with the place,

The Log of the Reine D'Avor

November 1938 **Friday 18**

It rained all day,
G. & I rowed punt to harbour for stores,
some damn row, G. got Paraffin Oil mixed in Sugar,
too bad for us,
B (Brache) family gone ashore all day to invite from some people, good for us,

We could have a good swear, better for us I stop aboard all day, Cook?

G., A. and I went fishing in evening, fed fish, no luck

The Log of the Reine D'Avor

November 1938   **Saturday 19**

G., A. & I went to town, and what a darn day, rain all day.

We call in at the Yacht Club, we are members for our stay here,
We had a drink, it's a fine Club,
from there to the Sailor's Rest, fine old place.
then to town, the boys shopped, then to the Bridgetown Club, fine big club,

When in town, local chaps call after the boys, 'who rob the barber', they make some fun,

Came back to ship on bus, which should have been a boat for the amount of water it went through on beach, and sang out to ship for an hour, frighten everything for a mile around; it rained like hell, got back to shore feeling like ****

                           ... a   perfect   day
(final log entry in diary)

The Log of the Reine D'Avor

Back page of diary:

Mr G H Harris – (George)
Emperor Goldmining Co Vatukoula,
Suva, Fiji Islands, South Pacific Ocean,

Mr A Kennard – (Arthur)
c/o Post Office,
Suva, Fiji Islands, South Pacific Ocean,
(and)

A E Kennard
89 High St
Worthing, Sussex

The Log of the Reine D'Avor

Postscript

Fred Rebell continued aboard the 'Reine D'Avor with the Brache family to Sydney, Australia, via the Panama Canal, arriving on 15 December 1939; he took up citizenship & the natural role as lay-preacher for a full & content life. Fred Rebell 'sailed over life's horizon' in 1968.

Sid left the Reine D'Avor on arrival at Barbados, 16-11-38; George & Arthur continued to Fiji & Tony joined the crew of the 40-ton Cutter-rig 'Osgar Tybring', 10-10-38.

Sid Jobbins returned to the UK, & worked for Hawker Siddeley Aviation, Kingston, Surrey, UK as a Coppersmith on the prototype Hawker Harrier jet, & continued in aviation until retirement: ref. Sid's skill as a Coppersmith... see rear coverplate: a 'silver-plate' yacht, he completed in full rig: the Reine D'Avor – detailed in every part.

Sidney 'sailed over the wider horizon' in 2001, aged 90 years.

... thank you, dad.

The Log of the Reine D'Avor

References:

'Escape to the Sea' Fred Rebell - first published 1940 John Murray Ltd, London)

Gillian Fulloon, 'Rebell, Fred (1886-1968)'...Australian Dictionary of Biography, Volume 11, Melbourne University Press, 1988 – pp 345-346)

The Log of the Reine D'Avor

Prologue:

After reading the Log of the Reine D'Avor, we leave you with the diary's last pencilled entry: highlighting Sid & shipmates joy of challenge and human endeavour, which remains the primary mover for all: whether desk-bound, or stepping-out to confront nature's elements in the raw... *where would we be without them?*

> **'Came back to ship on bus, which should have been a boat for the amount of water it went through on beach, and sang out to ship for an hour, frighten everything for a mile around; it rained like hell,**
>
> **got back to shore feeling like ****...**
>
> **... a perfect day'**

[diary transcribed verbatim from pencilled original; manuscript copy & all photos ©SidsSailingDays 2016]

The Log of the Reine D'Avor

The Log of the Reine D'Avor

Well Done to the family Brache & the crew…

The Log of the Reine D'Avor

Gallery: (some photos taken by the crew)

Fred Rebell, Sid & crew member outward-bound

The Log of the Reine D'Avor

A Fine yacht…

The Log of the Reine D'Avor

The Osgar Tybring

The Log of the Reine D'Avor

Harbour…

The Log of the Reine D'Avor

**In Harbour…
(Sid right… George, Arthur, Tony?)**

The Log of the Reine D'Avor

Fred Rebell & crew member in Harbour…

The Log of the Reine D'Avor

Yacht in Cancale Harbour

The Log of the Reine D'Avor

Sid & crew member in Habour…

The Log of the Reine D'Avor

Some of the family Brache & Sid

The Log of the Reine D'Avor

Sid's reverse photo terxt:

'October 20th 1938, next attempt,
Mr Rebell & myself repairing
Balloon jib, in The North East Trades,
About 300 miles from
Barbados, West Indies.'

The Log of the Reine D'Avor

'...repairing the staysail after she blew out in the Caribbean Sea'.

The Log of the Reine D'Avor

The Log of the Reine D'Avor

The crew of the Osgar Tybring in port?

The Log of the Reine D'Avor

The Gaff Rig…

The Log of the Reine D'Avor

...reminder of the old 'sea-dog' days'

The Log of the Reine D'Avor

Model: The Reine D'Avor crafted by Sid: all rigging, sails, hull…even to the crest of the waves – skill of the coppersmith set in 3-D ☺

The Log of the Reine D'Avor

Model: Reine D'Arvor -

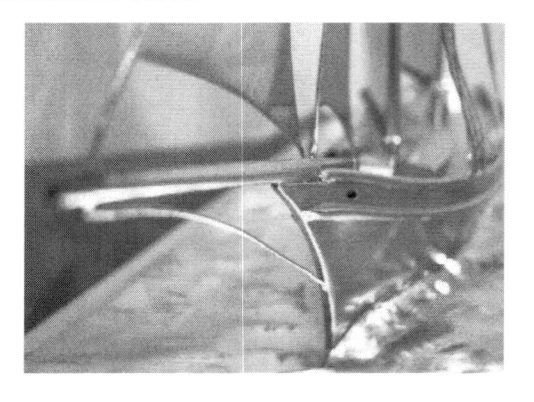

The Log of the Reine D'Avor

The Log of the Reine D'Avor

The Log of the Reine D'Avor

THANK YOU FOR SAILING WITH SID ...

The Log of the Reine D'Avor

Visit us @ www.SidsSailingDays.com

©Sid'sSailingDays2016

~~~~ooOOoo~~~~

The Log of the Reine D'Avor